How to Build Your Own Guitar

By

Glad Schwesinger

ISBN: 0-7596-9422-2 (softcover)
ISBN: 0-7596-9421-4 (ebook)

This book is printed on acid free paper.

1stBooks - rev. 2/25/02

INTRODUCTION

Our project shall be the nylon string Spanish guitar, one of the finest instruments of all time. This is an instrument with a pleasing tone and oh so fine to sing along with. The guitar does seem to enhance and improve each and every singer.

MATERIALS NEEDED

You shall need a few woodworking tools. One tool you shall positively need is a bending iron. The bending iron is used to heat wood. Wood which is very wet can be bent with heat, enough heat to make steam. My bending iron is a short piece of aluminum pipe of about three inch diameter and twelve inch length. I have an electric heating element inside the pipe but it could be heated with a torch. Be careful of fire. Do not use iron pipe as it will stain the wood black and spoil your job. Be sure to have a bit of patience and let the pipe get hot. If you try to bed wood without heat you will simply break the wood. Sides and strips I am going to bend are soaked in water for twenty four hours or more prior to bending. Factories have large heated molds but we can not afford that and I personally like the heating iron. With a bit of patience it does a good job.

FOLLOWING IS A TOOL LIST

Heating iron for bending pipe
Carpenter hammer
Crosscut hand saw
Small back saw to cut for frets
Jack plane and block plane
A few sharp chisels such as 1/2"
and a large 3/4"

I use the large chisel to trim braces on face board, if you can then find an old fashioned large chisel. You will find the weight is of much help, steadier to use.

Small doweling jig for drilling for tuning heads.

Rulers are a must—I use short 6", a 6' tape and yard stick.

Moto tool to do inlay, also to cut out sound hole.

Four sided rasp is a must with small and large cutters.

One round rasp—handy tool in corners.

Wood scraper, keep it sharp. I use wood scraper constantly. It is better than sand paper in many cases. I made my own scraper of an old metal saw blade. That steel holds a sharp edge and when finally dull I just use the grinder to quickley put on a new sharp edge.

Files—one long, at least twelve inch file, short flat file and a three corner file. Very small files, needle set to file notches for strings.

Side cutters to cut fret wire.

Screw drivers, both straight and Phillips.

One very small screw driver to set screws in tuning heads.

Clamps, wood clamps, C clamps, clamps can be home made from thin plywood. Cut long enough for wooden wedges to be used for pressure.

I keep a shoe box of clothes pins in shop.

Many clamps are needed, guitar supply shops sell large wooden clamps that are ideal for the job.

A wood vise and a regular bench vise Electric drill for bit up to 3/8" and set of bits.

Wood bit to 5/8" size to cut slots in head, You may prefer 1/2" size Oil stone for sharpening tools and electric grinder for same purpose.

Hack saw may be needed.

FOR POWER TOOLS I HAVE

Table saw
Small band saw
Drill press
Router

Electric sander, some jobs I prefer a sharp scraper.

It is quite possable to do some of these jobs by hand, it just take longer and more muscle.

Some work for which I have not the tools needed then I go to a local wood shop and hire the job done. Thus I have wood planed 3/32" thick. It would take too much time and work to do this by hand although I have made a setup to do this with a router. It still took too much time, I find it best to have a good wood shop do this job. Some quilted Maple did chip so easily that I had it sanded to 3/32" in a local wood shop with a power sander.

WOOD NEEDED

This guitar shall have a twenty five inch scale. That is the length from nut to bridge shall be exactly twenty five inches. Other scales are used but I like this scale and it is best to know the scale that will be used before the job is started. Farther along when it is time to saw for frets for fingerboard I shall give the complete scale.

SOUND BOARD

Sound board and braces shall be quarter sawn Spruce.

Boards—2—22" x 81/2" x 3/32"
Braces—2—12" x 3/4" x 1/4"
      6—12" x 1/4" x 3/16" # 6 is spare

HOW WILL WE GET A QUALLITY SOUND BOARD

To build a good guitar with good tone we need a good sound board. How does one get such a board? There are different ways. You may buy boards from a guitar supply shop. There are a few folks selling old growth Sitka Spruce blocks. If you can find and buy a good block, then you can split boards off. Notice, I said (split). Factories can not afford the waste so they saw boards. A saw does not care about the grain of the wood. A saw just does it's saw thing and does it very well. However, a good sound board must follow the grain of the wood and the only way to do that is to split boards off of a block. There are still a few old growth Spruce trees being sold. Years ago I bought a large block on the Oregon coast. This block I hand split boards from and had these boards planed to proper thickness. There was tremendous waste. I did however get perfect sound boards. Each board had quarter sawn grain and there was no cross grain going end ways of the boards. Small pieces were used for braces and here again were hand split. Then I put them through table saw using split edge as guide for first saw cut. Good old growth Sitka Spruce, knot free, vertical grain, makes very good tone wood.

Glad Schwesinger

HAND SPLITTING A SOUND BOARD FROM A
BLOCK. ALSO SOUND BOARDS MAY BE
PURCHASED FROM GUITAR SUPPLIERS

WITH FRO CONTINUE SLPITTING

BACK

Back and braces are hardwood—well matched slash grain looks nice.

Boards...2—22" x 8 1/2" x 3/32"
Braces...1—15" x 3/4" x 5/16"
          2—11" x 3/4" x 5/16"

Sides hardwood to match back...slash grain will bend easier. Note—face board must be quarter sawn and sides must be slash. You can see what I mean if you just take a deck of cards and bend them with your hands. Now stand them up and try to bend them the other way.

If you think on this you will soon see what I mean when I say quarter sawn grain and slash grain. Cheap factory guitars have the grain painted on the face but if you use a dentist type mirror and a small flashlight then you can look inside the guitar and see the true grain of the wood.

NECK BOARD

Neck…board is hardwood, I use Honduras Mahogany. This wood is easy to buy of nice straight grain and it is easy to work.

Board…1—36" x 3" x 1"

FRET BOARD

Fret board is very hard hardwood. Ebony was in the past standard but now it is hard to get good Ebony so most factory guitars have Maple that is stained black. I Use a hard wood which I buy from a local hardwood company. It may not be the best but it is available. I have used Ebony on a few guitars and I like it. The Ebony I used was purchased from a guitar supply shop.

Board…1—18" x 3" x 1/4"

Soft wood will be needed for mold and for liners. Clear fir or Pine, what is available.

OTHER MATERIALS NEEDED

Glue…Titebond

Fret wire…One 48" piece—why not buy more for your next guitar?

Tuning heads…One set—I like gold color

Bone…One bridge and one nut, A local music store should have them, they are very high priced

Sand paper…Several sheets from 80 grit to 400

Clear shellac…One small can

Alcohol thinner…One small can

Brush…One 2" brush

TIME TO START BUILDING

Sound Board

We have two boards 22" x 81/2" x 3/32" thick. These boards must be quarter sawn Spruce. We need a perfect straight edge on each board where they glue together. I check for smallest grain and mark these edges to be joined. That will be center of finished guitar. I use the table saw to make these edges perfectly straight and square. Set the guide so you cut off only one eighth inch or so on one side of each board. Now move guide just a bit for smaller board and cut other side. Move guide again for just a bit smaller and cut first side again. Presto, You have perfect edge and so simple. Do not angle saw nor try to complicate job. Just keep it simple. Use table saw guide as that should be perfectly straight. Now to glue these two boards together you will need a nice flat board large enough for both pieces to lie on side by side. Put wax paper on board where joint will be so you do not glue the pieces to work board. Next fasten one board so it does not slide about, use any small clamp. Apply Titebond glue to other board. Put two boards together and rub one back and forth to distribute glue. I often put a straight heavy straight edge on board close to joint just to make sure they lie flat and true. Put small pressure on second board with your hands just to make sure they are a snug fit. Now do not clamp any pressure on these boards. I repeat, - do not use any

USING TABLE SAW TO MAKE STRAIGHT EDGE
FOR GLUING ON SOUND BOARD

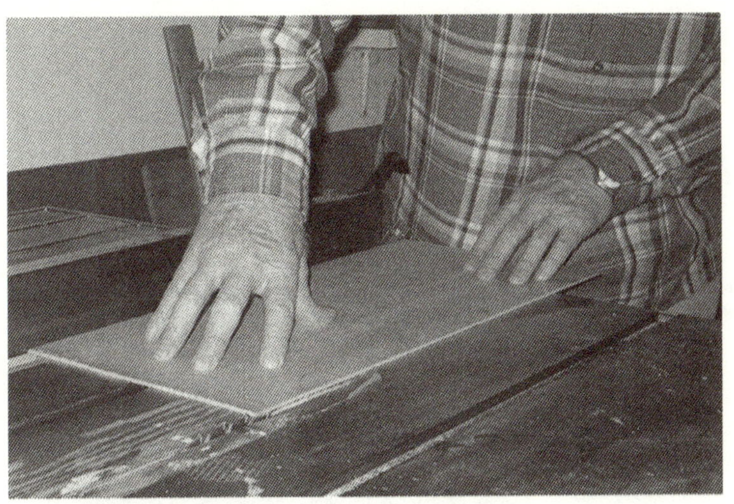

Glad Schwesinger

ONE BOARD ON WAX PAPER—GLUE APPLIED TO SECOND BOARD

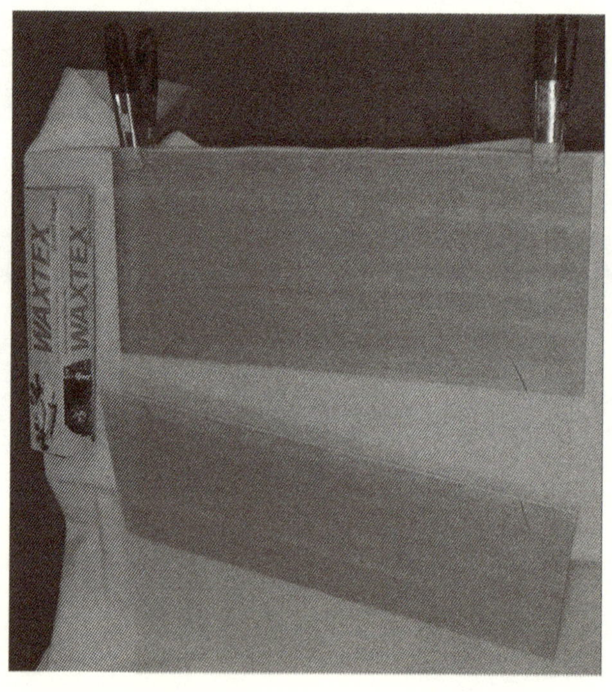

SOUND BOARDS READY FOR GLUE

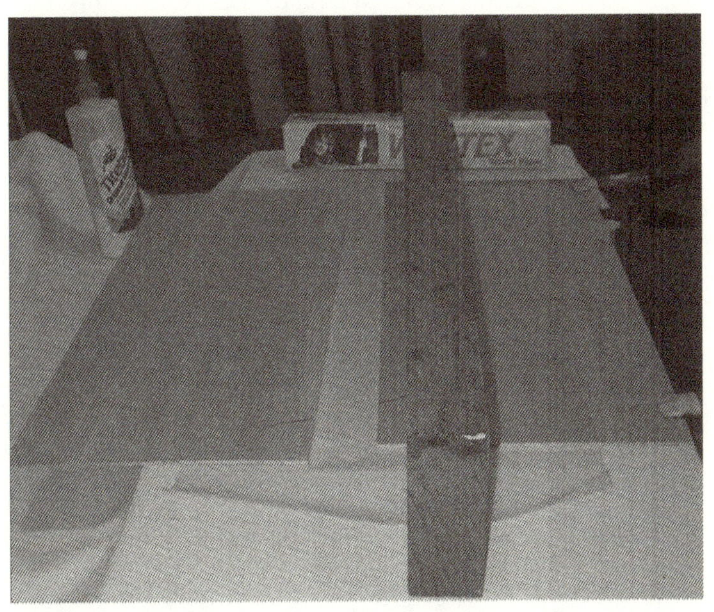

Glad Schwesinger

SOUND BOARDS GLUED—STRAIGHT EDGES HOLD
BOARDS DOWN—STRAIGHT EDGES REMOVED IN
TEN MINUTES. GLUE WILL PULL JOINT TIGHT
TRUST ME—NO CLAMPS

clamps for pressure on these boards. As the glue dries it will pull these boards together and make a very tight joint. Just trust me, do not use any clamps as that will pull boards out of line and cause trouble. Next day this board will be strong enough to work with. Keep this board where it will continue to dry as we need all of the moisture out of this face board before we glue the braces on. If we have shrinkage after the guitar is built we shall have a guitar with a cracked face. Find a place where this board will dry and leave it set for a spell. A good place to dry a board is to lean it against an inside wall where the air will dry the wood. Winter time when the furnace is heating is ideal time for this and be sure to use inside wall.

BACK

Here we also have two boards 22" x 8 1/2" x 3/32". The same method is used for back as was used for face board. Alternately put these boards through table saw to make a tight fit. Then on same work board use wax paper to keep from sticking to work board and glue these two boards together. Hold one board in place with small clamp. Apply glue to other board and place two boards together, again rub them a bit to make sure glue is on all surface to be joined and use hands to give just a bit of pressure. Again I use two large straight pieces set on these boards to keep them flat and even. Again I say, use no clamps. The glue will pull these boards together, trust me—no clamps. This board must be left to dry and be sure it is very dry before braces are glued on as we do not want a guitar with a cracked back. Use heat if needed but get board dry.

OUTSIDE MOLD

While we wait we can build an outside mold. Some Luthiers do not use a mold and do not believe in a mold but I use one and if properly used I consider it a good way to do the job. Scrap wood can be used to make the mold. Make a paper pattern for one half. Use this pattern to mark both sides and then they should be exactly the same. I mark the paper out in one inch squares. One side is center, here is marked the length of sound box. Width of large bout is marked and width at waist of instrument is marked. Now width of small bout is marked. Now with a soft pencil a line is drawn connecting these points. Look at your work and make it pleasing to the eye. Go to town and look at a few guitars to see what looks good to you and try to copy. I keep both ends straight for just a bit so end blocks can be straight. Now freehand I draw the line and adjust it until it looks good. Now use this pattern to mark the wood for the mold. I saw these boards in the band saw but if you have no band saw then it can be done with a key hole saw and smoothing with a rasp. This mold should be about two inches deep and held together on each end with a thin plywood board. I have used screws so I can take mold apart if needed. I used layers of wood, 3/4" scrap fir glued together and smoothed with a wood rasp. Do not get the idea to make a far different shape nor to give the box more shape. I have tried many different patterns and made the neck end much smaller but it did not make a better guitar. I do make the neck end a bit smaller just for looks, not for sound. I did try one time to turn the box around as we can see when looking at a horn the sound starts out where it is small and comes out where it is large. When I got this odd guitar built it was so awkward to hold and play that I just cut it up and threw it on the burning pile. Keep it simple. We need a size for this guitar. My favorite of all the nylon string guitars I have made has a width at large bout of almost 15", a waist of 10&1/2" and a lower bout of 11". Do not make the waist smaller, it would be better to change it to larger if you change it any. I mean a 10&3/4" waist might be better. Easier to bend the sides and enough indent to rest the guitar on the knee in comfort. This guitar has a box 19" long. The sound hole center is five and one quarter inches from the end of small bout with a diameter of three and one half inches. I have at times placed the sound hole closer to the end of small bout with the desire to create a larger surface of sound board to vibrate. I really have not been able to say it was better. A small amount of change will not adversely effect the instrument which means the shape of a good guitar is not written in stone and can vary just a bit. Try to use common sense and make it pleasing to the eye.

MOLD DIMENSIONS ARE AS FOLLOWS

Length.................................... 19"
Width at small bout .... 11"
Width at waist........................ 10 1/2"
Width at large bout.................... 15"
Sound hole size......................3 1/2"

Mark these on pattern for future use.

BENDING THE SIDES

Cut boards for size before bending. These boards are 32" long, 4" wide at wide end, and 3 3/4" at small end or even just a bit smaller. The face side should be left straight. The back side is on a taper. Some builders taper the small.

Glad Schwesinger

BENDING SIDE BOARD OVER HOT PIPE

CHECKING BEND ON MOLD

Glad Schwesinger

ONE SIDE BENT—CLAMPED IN MOLD

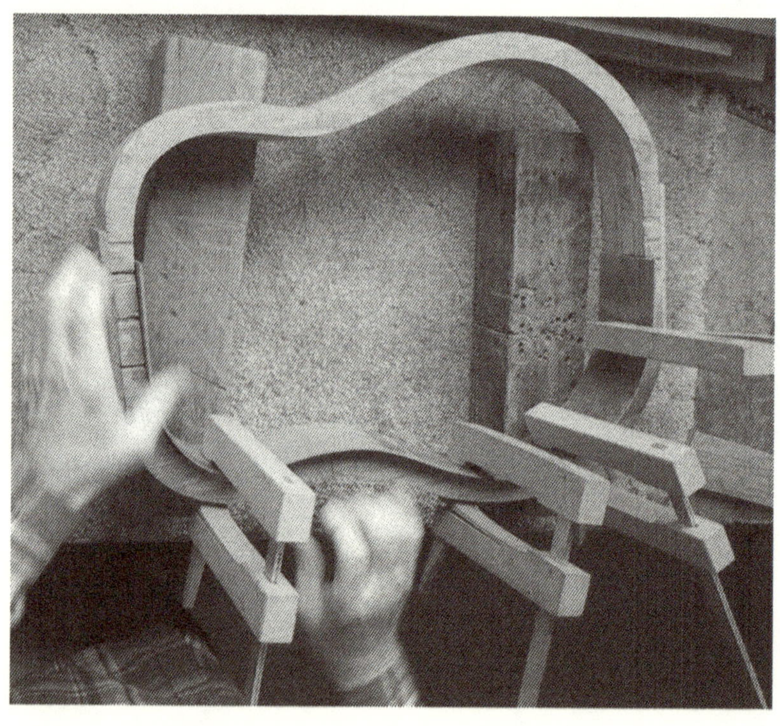

BOTH SIDES CLAMPED IN MOLD

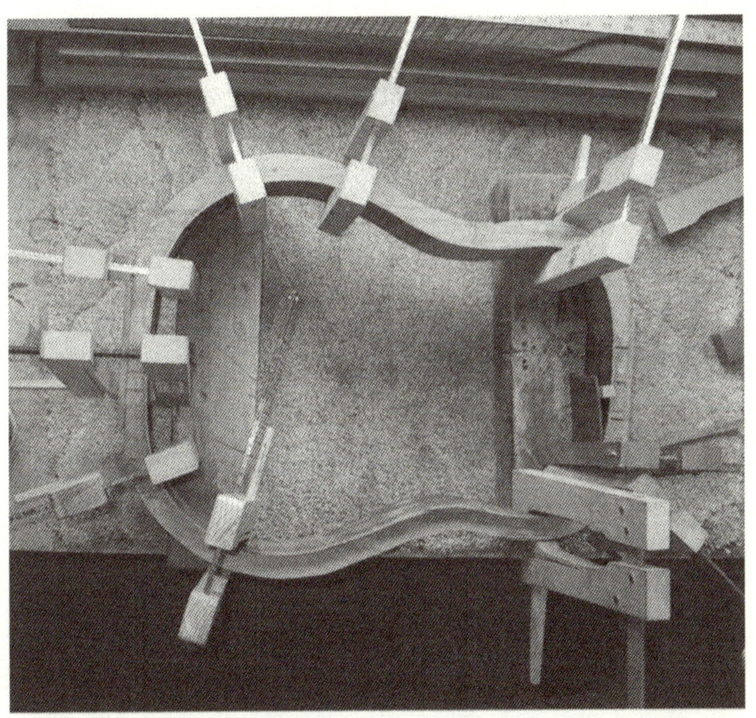

Glad Schwesinger

BLOCKS GLUEDAT EACH END

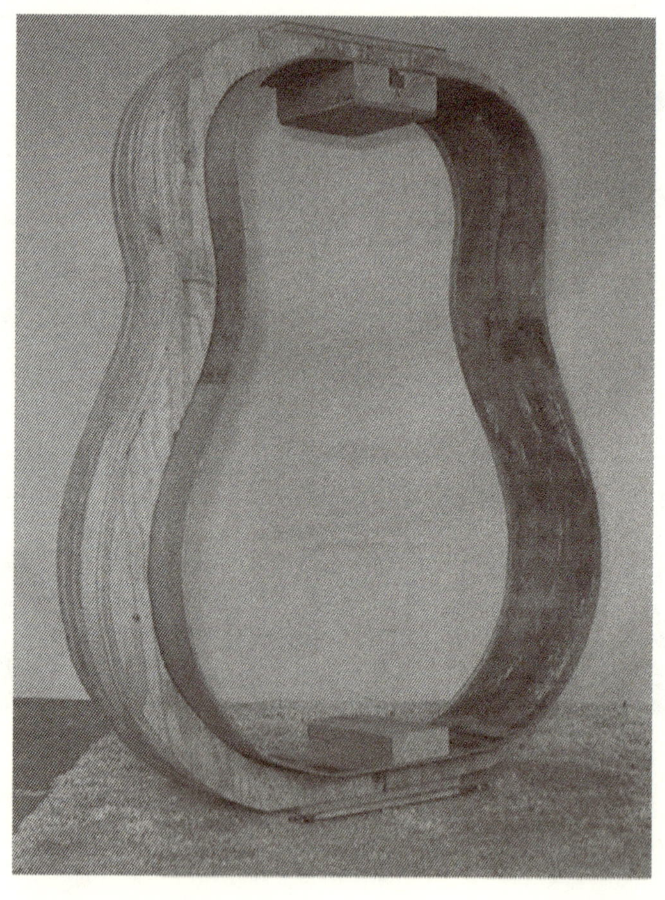

WORK BOARD WITH HOLE FOR CLAMP

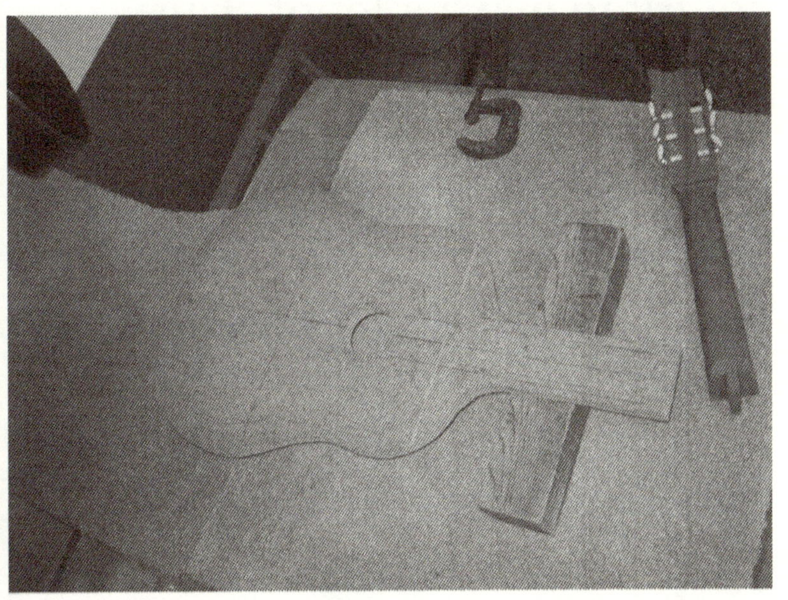

end just a bit more from the center of curve to center of mold. This is done for looks, not for sound. Do not try to make a lot of shape for if it were even it would be easier to put together. I have made sides both wider and narrower but a four inch deep box is quite standard and does seem to have the best balance. A deeper box will have more base. For chords only and to sing along that might be better. These are things best left for future guitars. Your first guitar is best kept standard. The builder can stop by a music store and check a few guitars, take a ruler with and check which ones take your eye and your ear. While you are looking do not get confused with a steel string guitar as that is an animal of a different father. I set mold up close to bending iron and try to bend sides to fit mold. This job is of utmost importance. Keep with it until sides are a good fit. I know that sides can be clamped to the mold but that is not the way to do. The builder must keep working until sides fit mold and then use clamps just to hold sides in mold. Sides should be well marked for sound board side and a square cut made where they are to be joined at center of large bout. One way to get perfect fit is to lay boards out on straight edge with ends overlapped just a bit. Then cut both ends at the same time. This can be done on the table saw or it can be done with a router or even a sharp hand saw. Another way to get perfect fit is to cut ends at an angle, clamp them to block and cut wedge shaped piece to fit. I have made wedge of different color wood and it can look very nice. Whichever way it is done now is the time to make a small block, a block to fit the sides and thick enough to hold a pin for a guitar strap if one wishes to have one latter. Glue the sides to this block. I find it is best to put wax paper on a very smooth flat surface and glue and clamp them together. When the glue has set I put sides back in mold. Now the sides can be cut at other end with just a bit of clearance so they do not touch each other. Now I need to make a block with about a half inch square slot for the neck to fit into. This block will be easier to make if the instrument has very little taper. Cut it for correct length, center it on the mold. Mark where it goes. Now it should be glued and clamped in place. Remember, when you are gluing, wax paper will keep things from sticking to the mold. I prefer to line the sides, sound board side down, on a very flat smooth surface. The end blocks if properly cut will set on the surface and it is an easy alignment. A few clamps will hold sides in mold and one

clamp will hold end block in place
while glue sets.

SIDES KEEP SHAPE WITHOUT USE OF MOLD VERY IMPORTANT

Glad Schwesinger

OUTSIDE MOLD—USED TO MARK FACE AND BACK BOARD AND TO HOLD SIDES WHILE FACE IS GLUED ON

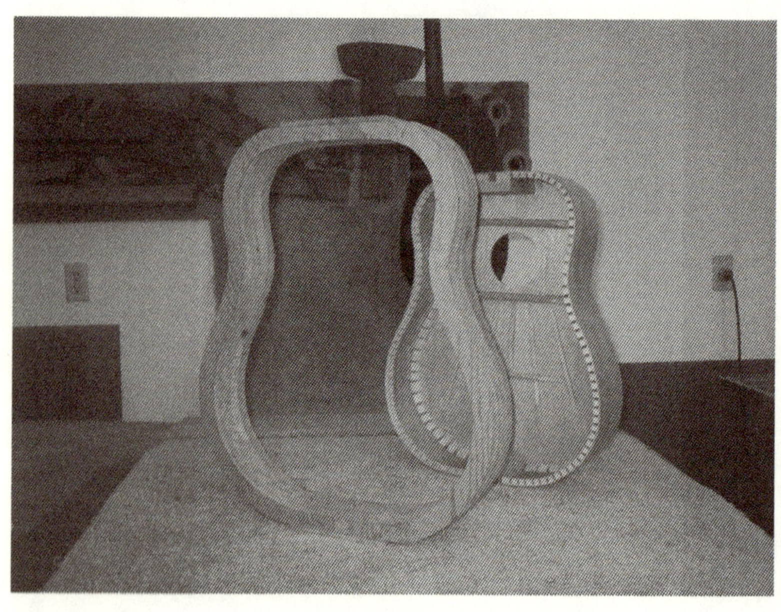

MORE ASSEMBLY

While the back is drying we can work on the face. The mold is used to mark the shape of the guitar. Center of sound hole is marked. Here I drill a quarter inch hole. Now with moto router I can cut groove for inlay around sound hole. I use the same flat board that was used for joining the face boards but now I will drill a hole in this board with a quarter inch bit. The center hole in the face must be lined with this hole and a quarter inch bit in a guide block on the router will guide the router on a true circle as groove is cut for inlay. It is an easy job, just go slow and careful, job is soon done. Now a strip of wood must be cut that will fit the groove and this strip must be bent with the heating pipe in a small enough circle to fit in the groove. After it is glued in place I leave it with a weight on it for glue to set. After glue has set I use block plane and scraper to cut surplus wood off down even with face board. Note, you are not trying to fit a paper thin wood into a groove. A large piece of wood is so easily fitted in groove and surplus is trimmed off before sound hole is cut out. The finished inlay looks hard to do but is really quite

MOTO TOOL CUTTING FOR INLAY AROUND SOUND HOLE

Glad Schwesinger

INLAY WOOD WAS SHAPED WITH HOT PIPE NOW READY TO GLUE IN PLACE

INLAY SMOOTHED FLUSH WITH SOUNDBOARD
SOUND HOLE CUT OUT WITH SAME MOTO TOOL
AFTER INLAY IS SMOOTHED DOWN REMEMBER
AFTER INLAY IS SMOOTH

easy. Old standard way they made a fancy purfling to go around sound hole but remember, we are trying to make this job easier. After this job is finished then the sound hole is cut out. With a bit of adjustment the same router is used to cut this three and one half inch hole.

BRACING FOR SOUND BOARD

Lines for layout of braces should be marked on inside of sound board. I will show different types of bracing. They are very similar and all do well. The builder can decide which type to use. The first method shall be of a bracing that has one cross brace at an angle. The

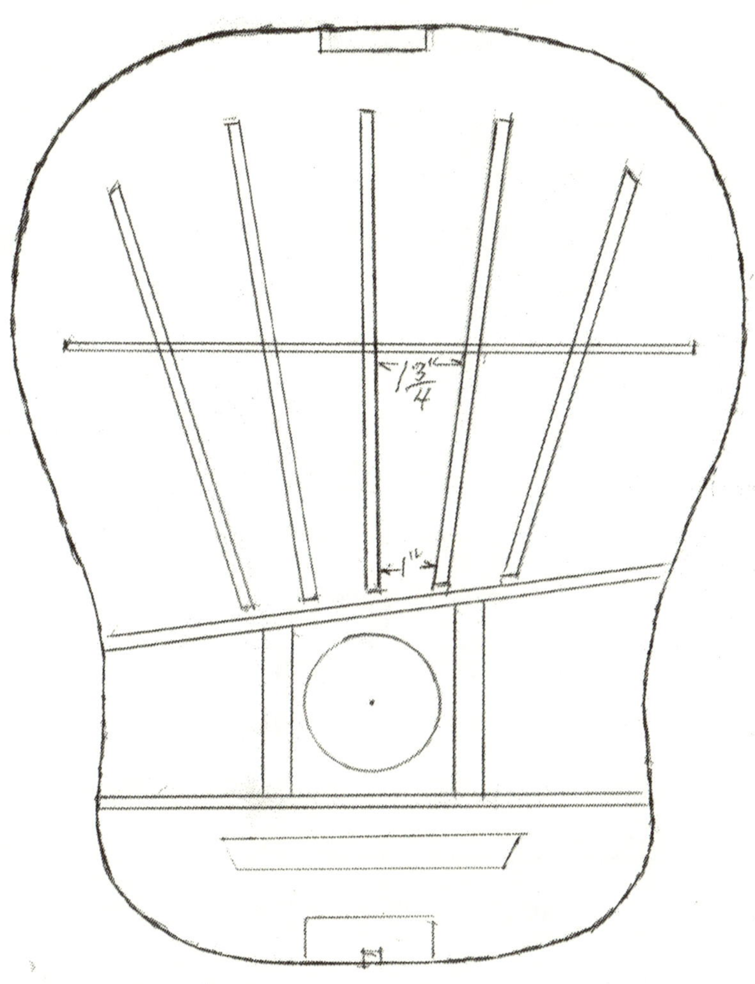

1 3/4"
1"

cross brace next to the sound hole shall be placed so as to shorten the fan bracing on the high note side and have longer braces for the bass side. This was done by a famous guitar builder in England many years ago. I did try it and I did like it. This guitar had a small brace under bridge which went almost to sides of guitar. This brace was quarter sawn Spruce 1/4" wide, 3/8" high under center and tapered down at ends. I shall show pictures of cross braces and of fan braces. For bracing on each side of sound hole I used scrap from the face board. Thus those braces are wide and thin. Also brace under finger board was of same material, wide and thin. This shows that heavy bracing is not needed in most parts of instrument. Understand also, a million guitars have been built with cross braces square across, it is the builders choice. Another way to balance a guitar is as follows—before it is finished, that is before the face is finished put the strings on and tune the instrument. Then proceed to use a sharp scraper to remove wood from the bass side. When I say bass side I mean side next to your nose as you pay this instrument. Listen to it, do not take off too much. You can hear the bass improve. If you have a good sound board the high notes will sound good, It is the bass where you need some help. I have seen many complicated styles of bracing but mostly they are just a wild dream. Keep the bracing simple. The cross bracing next to the sound hole must be strong enough to keep the instrument from caving in. Once you understand that then you will see the fan bracing should be very small. Cross braces are one quarter inch thick, three quarter inch wide and long enough to reach across face. Quarter sawn Spruce is best. I plane them wedge shaped and trim down the ends just to eliminate wood. Wood will absorb sound so we want no surplus of heavy wood sticks. I put a very sight curve on the side which glues to the face board, not much, just a sixteenth or so, I do not want face to have a hollow look. After finish is on guitar must cure. It will be a month or more before the tone is there so do not get in a hurry to judge your work. Give It time. Now I wish to show a different style of bracing. Cross bracing is much the same but we will cut out wood on the side of brace next to face board. About one inch from center to about one inch from edge of instrument. This is done on each side. Now there is room for fan bracing to pass under cross braces. The theory is to allow more of face board to vibrate. I have the feeling it lets more of the board adjust to weather change such as dry and damp. Years ago when traveling to Arizona each winter I found that guitars did suffer with prolonged dry hot air conditions. A man by the name of Bouchet came up with this idea. Recent years Arthur Overholtzer did much the same thing. On these braces I also have put just a bit of curve as I did not want the face to have a hollow look. Also the curve makes the instrument stronger. I glue cross braces on first. I use clamps to hold them tight to face board. Now braces can be cut for the fan bracing. Again we need quarter sawn Spruce. These pieces are 3/16" wide and 1/4" high and long enough to reach from 1/2" of cross bracing to 3/4" of edge. Some builders prefer these strips to be higher. To all you beginners, the grain must be up and down. Braces are much stronger that way. Here again I like just a bit of curve, so little that I just rub the end part on sand paper a few strokes just to make sure the face board is not hollow when finished. These strips can be glued in place and trimmed with a sharp chisel after the glue is dry. However I do find it a good idea to cut some of the shape on the band saw before gluing them on. As the work progresses you can tap the board for sound. Hold the board up with one finger through the sound hole and tap where the bridge will be. You must try to balance the need to vibrate with the need for strength. Too much wood can hinder the volume of instrument as it both hinders and

absorbs sound. When you feel that the fan braces are small enough then see if you can make them still smaller. Now I want to tell you just what we are trying to do. A good sound board is the correct balance of weight and strength. Spruce is very strong for the weight of wood. The brace next to sound hole on bridge side is the brace that will need to be super strong. That is the brace that will keep the face from caving in. Notice size of that brace. On neck side of sound hole is brace that will keep the fret board from pushing sound board in. When this is understood then it becomes apparent that the fan bracing may be very small and very simple.

Many modern builders are inclined to have no bracing under bridge. This method does eliminate weight. So here we are, back to strength enough with a minimum of weight. I have tried many systems of fan bracing but small and light and simple is best.

BACK BRACING NEEDED

Next I work on the back. The outline is marked by placing mold on back and drawing line all the way around. Braces now may be cut for the back. These are usually hardwood but can be spruce. Some builder use four braces but I find three to be adequate. Here also I wish them to have a curve. The back can have more curve than the face, I taper them 1/4" or even more. I have laid out a line with the curve I want on a small board. I use this to draw a line on the braces. I have done this because I have continued building instruments and use the same pattern over and over. Having marked the braces I now lie them flat on a smooth surface, carefully pick up all three, put them in the vice and plane them all three at the same time. That way they all have the same curve. I like the looks of the curved back. These braces also must be kept as small as what will do the job. I plane them wedge shape and taper the ends down to 1/4" high. Remember, extra wood just absorbs sound. To hold center joint very thin wood is cut with grain of wood going across and glued on between the braces. This thin wood will curl up from water it absorbs from the glue. Therefore one must use weight or clamps to hold this wood while glue sets. These pieces are about one inch wide and very thin, like cardboard and need to be rounded on edges just for looks when friends peek in the sound hole. When I am gluing them in I often put a drop of water on opposite of glue side just to keep them flat as glue sets. Many builders will now give complete instructions for fitting the ends of braces into side lining. This is a difficult job and because we are tying to make this job easier we shall consider two easy ways to do this job. First way is—just cut braces short of side lining and taper down to nothing. Very easy, very quick. Another way is, have sides in mold. Fit sides to back. Be sure it is good fit. Now set back down on two blocks. Set sides, still in mold on back. Now before face board is on it is so simple to place small blocks on cross braces. Just put a bit of glue on blocks. Careful, do not get any glue on back as we must remove back to fasten face. Think about this, you are just working in a very shallow box. Hold back to sides with clamps. Hold these small blocks with a finger until glue takes a hold. Later you have face glued on and neck glued on and you go to set back you will find you have perfect fit on these blocks and need only add glue as back is glued on. I find the table saw is a fine place to work at fitting back to sides and face to sides as I am able to walk all around and check all sides. Most work benches are against a wall and thus there is no way to check one side. Just roll the saw blade down and here is smooth flat surface to work on. When glue has set on blocks is a good time to admire your work and then set this back board aside until sound board and sides are joined and neck is set and fastened solid in place.

SIDES AND SOUND BOARD ARE SECURED

Again a smooth flat surface is best. Place sound board down with braces up. You will need very small wedges to put under edges of board to hold it steady as board as made with a curve. Now set sides, still in mold, on sound board. Builder can look to see if there is a fit. If not then builder must mark and plane off high spots until there is a good fit. When a good fit is made then is time to glue sides and face board together. I make and use small blocks for this job. To make these blocks I cut strips of softwood about two feet long. These strips are about five sixteenth thick and one quarter inch wide. I then set band saw to cut them wedge shaped. Now square up the saw table and cut small blocks from these strips. Blocks are from one half inch to five sixteenth inch long. When I have enough of these I put glue on end blocks and set sides back face board. Now I glue blocks in one at a time. Put glue on block and hold it in place for just a bit. Remember, no great pressure. If the builder is careful the sides and face board are glued together with no undue stress on the wood. I like this method, it

FACE GLUED TO SIDES BY USE OF SMALL
BLOCKS—SUPPORT BLOCKS FOR BACK ARE IN
PLACE AS THEY WERE GLUED BEFORE

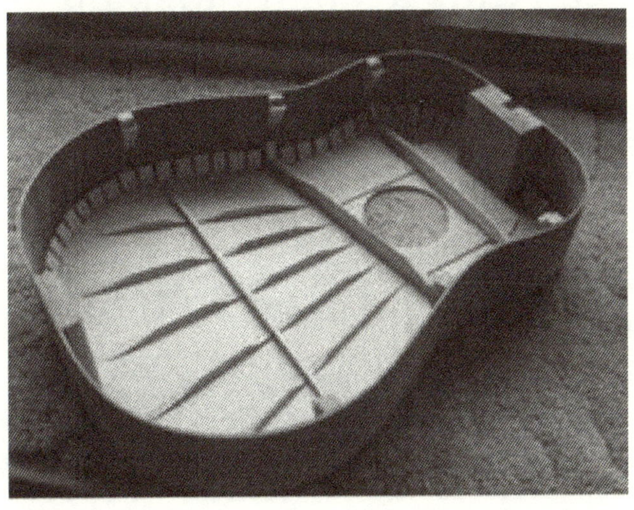

is so much better than clamping face to a strip which is already glued on sides. The cross braces should fit against the sides and now you can glue a small block on cross brace and side. Easy to make perfect fit this way. These four blocks will help strengthen the cross braces and done this way it is so easy to make perfect fit. Now the liner can be glued to sides for the back to fasten on. I make these liners much as I made blocks to fasten face board. Cut strips about two feet long. Use table saw to notch them with notches about one half inch apart and almost thru. I have plywood board that slides on saw and has straight edge on to hold material as I saw. I line several strips together and saw all at same time. Now I can check for a fit between blocks and cut for length and glue in place. Here is where I am going to use all those clothes pins. They are the perfect clamp to hold these strips on while glue sets. Remember, back was fitted to sides so keep these strips even with sides so back will still fit on blocks. If any of them are high you will need to rasp them down.

INLAY WHERE SIDES JOIN FACE BOARD

Surplus face board wood must be trimmed off. I use band saw, rasp and scraper. Now the box is ready to notch for inlay. I use wood. I like wood of a different color, either darker wood or a very light wood. I want a contrast with the sides. Store bought guitars have a plastic inlay. I like wood. Plastic is tone dead and it does seem all guitars are inlay with black and white. Do not even consider plastic as then you will just have a store bought looking guitar. You must keep to small inlay or use two or more strips of wood. Strips of different color look nice. I soak these strip in water.

And heat bend them to fit in the mold where I clamp them. Then I glue them on. I use masking tape to hold them. I use a lot of tape. Most builders use rubber bands but I like masking tape. I did at one time inlay both front and back but now I just inlay the front. On back I have same kind of wood and I rather like them without inlay when I have a good fit of the wood. With Rosewood I usually inlay both front and back but with Honduras Mahogany or Koa wood back and sides I like to join the wood. What inlay is done is not written in stone, a guitar could be built with no inlay. It would look well if the builder did a good job with tight fits. Also the guitar would sound good for the guitar is not a violin.

CUTTING FOR INLAY

BUILDING NECK IS MOSTLY A HAND JOB

The easy way is to buy a good hardwood board one inch thick, three inches wide and three feet long. I like Honduras Mahogany as it is so nice to work. Some builders like Rosewood because it is stronger and so they make a thinner neck. Now blocks can be cut from this board and glued to each end giving enough wood to band saw out a rough outline of the neck. There is another way to put a head on a neck by just sawing the board at an angle. Measure enough wood for the end and cut off at an angle of about seventeen degrees. Now you can glue this block to the long piece. Note, you should have these boards of the thickness you want to finish with before they are glued together. When you have the end glued on you can make sure it is smooth and ready for the trim that goes on top then it is time to measure for length and make the end cuts to fit it into box. I cut the end square and keep a one half inch tenon to fit into block at end of box. This joint must be made while wood is still all of same width. After that joint is done it is time to start to shape the neck. I band saw it very close to width. Then it must be finished with a wood rasp and a

block plane and sand paper. A
finish board is glued on the head. In

HEAD OF NECK—NOTCHES AND HOLES CUT

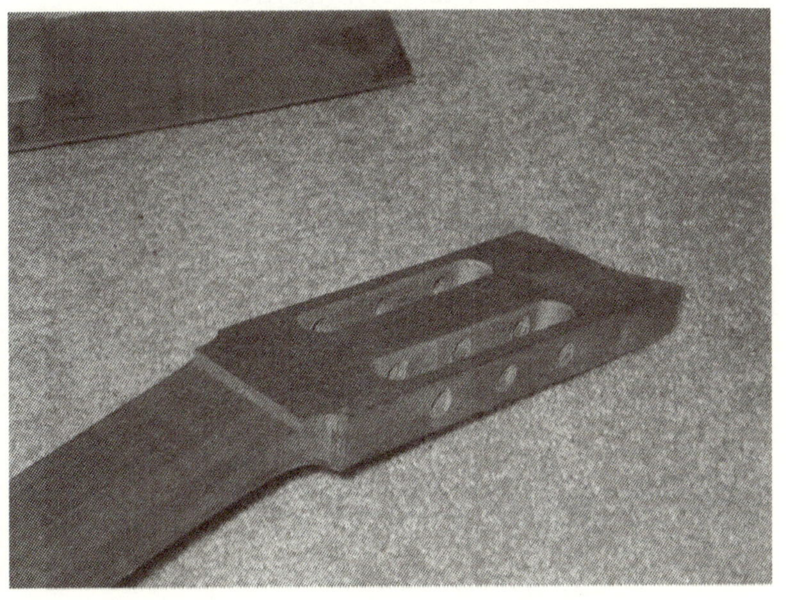

DRAWING SHOWS HOW NECK IS MADE
ROUNDING IS HAND JOB DONE MOSTLY WITH
WOOD RASP AND SCRAPER

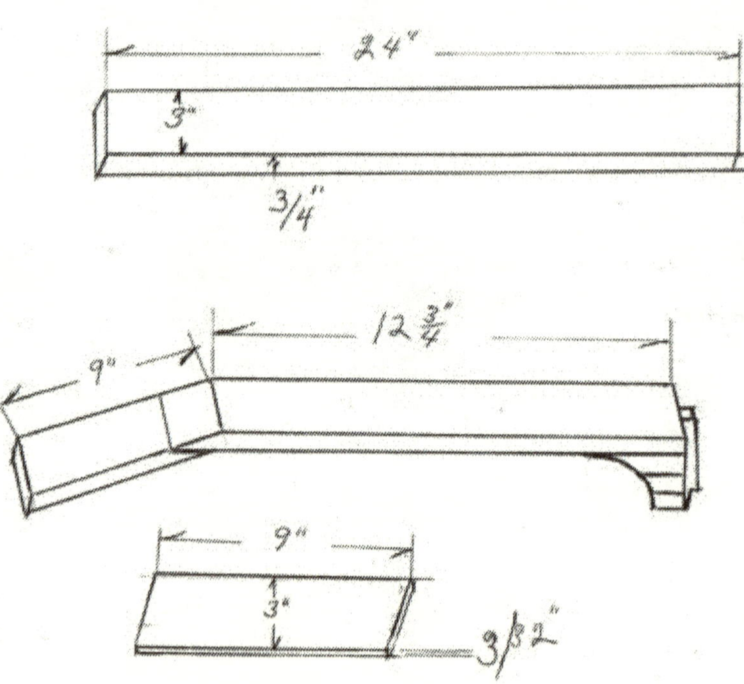

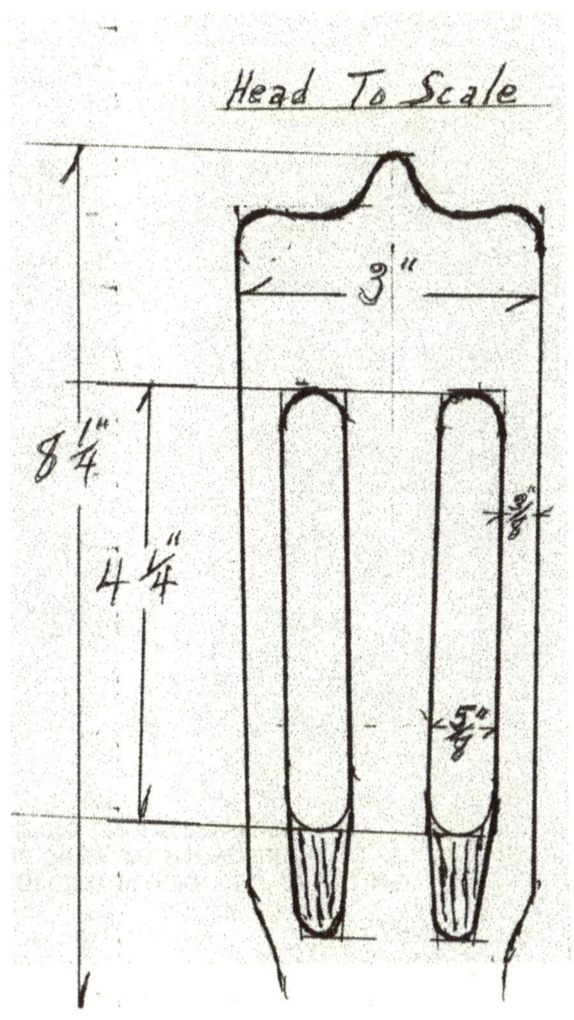

Head To Scale
3"
8 1/4"
4 1/4"
3/8"
5/8"

DOWLING JIG IN USE

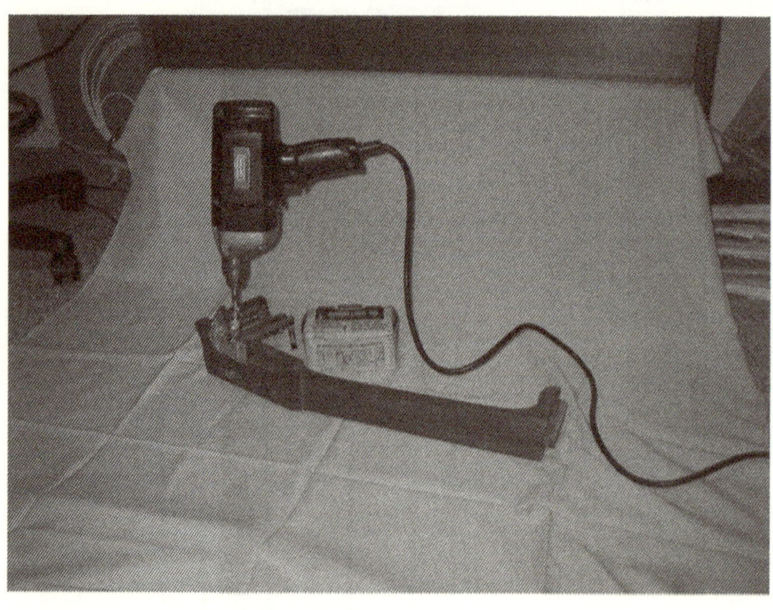

the past this has been a very thin board but I use wood of about three thirty seconds as I like the added strength. Slots for tuning heads are cut with a router or with several holes drilled in line and then the use of a keyhole saw and smoothed up with a rasp and sand paper. I use very small gouge to take out wood for strings to pass and I often put my name on by just using a pencil or ball point pen and then shellacking right over. I like it because it is so simple. I have bought letters that glued on and were finished over but like I say the pen is so simple to use. Just a bit of pressure as you go over the print will make an indent in the wood.

For drilling the holes for the rollers I have a doweling jig. This does such a good job that if you do not have one then you best go to the local hardware and purchase your own doweling jig. You had best purchase the tuning heads before you drill holes for them so you can be sure to make them fit. To have inlay full length of the neck I have just glued wood of different color together and then band sawed the proper shape. Making the neck is a great deal of work. I like to make the round have an angle out so I can make the finger board just a tiny bit narrower. Then when finger board is glued on I take a scraper to this extra wood on the neck and soon have perfect fit. The head I like to be eight and one half inches long. From where the nut is to where the neck fits into the box should be twelve and one half inches. That is just one half of the twenty five inch scale. Do not sweat this, it can vary just a tiny bit but when the bridge is set it must be exactly twenty five inches. The bridge is the last thing glued on and it must be right. Guitars are built both larger and smaller with scale to match but we started out to build to a twenty five inch scale and that is what we must stick with. Whatever size instrument the builder is working to the scale must be known in advance and that should be the scale worked to, no other way is possible. When you have the neck finished it will give you a great deal of satisfaction to look at and admire the fine work you have done.

NOW IS TIME TO FASTEN NECK TO BOX

For this job I have a work board that I made of particle board. The board is shaped like a guitar and has a hole to match sound hole in guitar. I set this board up on two four by fours. That gives me enough space to install a small C clamp through the sound hole. Because the face is slightly rounded I need a few small wood wedges to steady the box. The end where the neck fits in is pulled down tight to work board. Some fitting may need to be done here. When that is finished then builder must put wax paper under joint. Now glue is applied and a C clamp will draw them tight together. Here is where I use two screws to fasten this joint. If the builder is dead set against screws then just drill a quarter inch hole down one side of tenon and with glue on it insert a quarter inch dowel. Presto—that will lock the joint. Personally I like the screws. I have the neck clamped to the work board and centered and the screws will pull this joint snug and tight. I feel that the screws have no effect at all on the sound. Two wood screws are not going to make this box scream nor whistle nor any thing bad, you

NECK IS FASTENED TO BOX USING WORK BOARD

can not even see them when job is done.

LET US NOW INSTAL THE BACK

Work board is again in use. Clamp neck down on work board. Make sure it is centered and again use small C clamp through sound hole. Again use wood wedges to hold box firmly in position. Check back for fit and when you feel it is well fitted then it is time to apply glue. We need glue al around and on end blocks and on support blocks that were installed on sides. Make sure it is in position and clamp with large wood clamps and just very little pressure. When it looks O K then leave set while glue dries. Next day is time to trim off surplus wood and smooth the joint all around. Now builder can decide if inlay is to be used or if it is to be left as is. I say, when sides and back are matching wood and the joint is good then I like it without inlay.

A FRET BOARD IS NEEDED

Ebony is considered best but not only is it costly, it is becoming difficult to buy and most of what is on the market has some white streaks. Most store bought guitars have a hard maple fret board that is stained black. I have been using a hard wood which I buy from a local hard wood store and which I got in vertical grain. I know it is not as hard as ebony but it does a fair good job. This wood is I believe from Africa and it has one fault. Thinner brings out a red color which will stain other work if I am not careful. After I get it sealed with one coat of shellac my problem is over. We need a board in the rough of about two and three quarter inch wide, one quarter inch thick and about eighteen inches long. Slots for frets must be cut while this board is still even of sides. To do this job I made a miter box of hard maple. I made this box long enough to measure the entire board. Thus I have marks on bottom board to move fret board to for line up of each cut. I use a small back saw and I removed some of the set on the teeth with an oil stone so the frets would be a tight fit in the slots. For depth I clamp a strip of wood on saw blade to stop saw when correct depth is reached.

Make this miter box with care. This job is very important. I will now try to explain fret spacing and list measurements for fret spacing.

TIME TO MAKE FRET BOARD

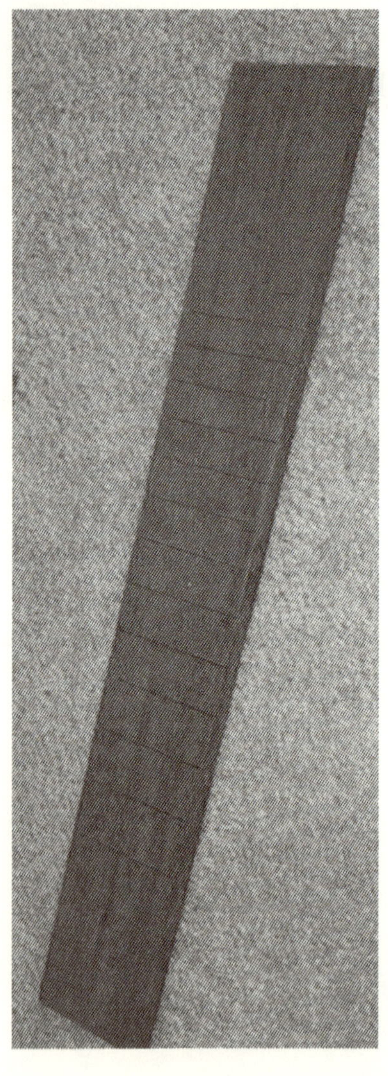

TIME TO MAKE FRET BOARD

WORK BOARD—USED WHEN GLUING SIDES TO
SOUND BOARD—WHEN FITTING AND FASTENING
NECK TO BOX AND WHEN FITTING AND GLUING
BACK ON BOX. HOLE AT SOUND HOLE POSITION
ENABLES USE OF SMALL CLAMP. BOARD WAS
MADE OF ¾" PARTICLE BOARD

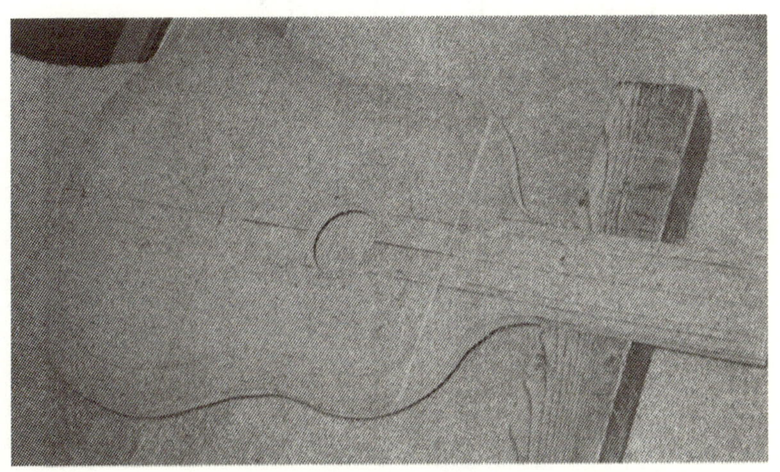

Glad Schwesinger

MEASURE FOR FRETS ON FRET BOARD

Fret # inches fret # inches

1...1 3/8" 11...11 3/4"
2...2 11/16" +1/32 12...12 1/2"
3...3 15/16" 13...13 3/16 + 1/32"
4...5 1/8" 14...13 15/16"
5...6 1/4" 15...14 9/16"
6...7 5/16" 16...15 1/8"
7...8 5/16" 17...15 11/16"
8...9 1/4"
9...10 1/8"
10...10 15/16"

Board must have one square end.
Check your marks very carefully.

You can see with eye if they are uniform as the spacing gets smaller. After all slots are cut you may now cut board to size. Board shall be two inches wide at nut end and two and three eighths where it is at box. That is fret # 12. Exact length may be gotten by placing board in position, then reaching in sound hole with short pencil and marking at edge of hole. I saw about one eighth shorter so I just cover inlay and leave a bit of face board showing. I have fretted the board and then installed it but it is better to glue it on neck and install frets after the board has been checked and made perfectly straight. Wise builders know that finger nails cut in and wear hollows in fret boards. For this reason they change to a simple cheap white glue for the fret board. In future years when board needs replacing the repair man need only to put a block of hard wood at end of finger board and with a sharp crack of a hammer the board is loose. That will make the repair job so much easier. After board is glued on make sure it is straight. Use scraper and long file and check it with straight edge. When you feel it is straight then it is time to install frets. A few firm taps with hammer on each fret. Do not hit hard, check each fret that it is down. When all are in the ends must be filed down even with the wood. These ends must be rounded off so the fingers slide along while playing. No musician wishes to cut a finger on a sharp fret. Now a long flat file may be used to double check the frets for even. A high fret may need only another tap with the hammer. I put masking tape on sound board next to fret board so I do not mark face board with file. This is a very important job so do it with care. One more small job on the fret board, between the sixth and seventh fret we need a small white marker so the musician knows what fret he is on. I did buy and install Mother of Pear. It is costly and most listening music lovers seldom even see these markers so I got wise. I buy knitting needles and cut off a short length with a hack saw. I drill for this piece and put it in the small hole with glue. When glue is set it is filed even and job is done. I like to put a thin coat of shellac on the instrument just to protect it from finger marks. The oil from fingers will mark bare wood. A thin coat of shellac will not interfere with work and will protect the wood.

MAKE AND INSTALL A BRIDGE

You had best go to the local music store and purchase the bone for the bridge. You will be shocked when they tell you the price and you may start to consider other material but do not go with plastic. Plastic is tone dead. Now you have the bone, next you need a good small piece of hardwood. Good guitars are usually Rosewood. I have used Myrtle wood. Years ago when I was visiting in Oregon I went to one of the shops making Myrtle wood objects to sell and bought a block of wood. I did like the wood and it can be stained to look like Rosewood or Mahogany or left natural. There are other hard woods that will do a good job. Look for wood that is hard and will carve well and not crack nor warp. A block of wood about eight inches long, one and one quarter inch wide and one half inch deep. First cut this wood down to 3/8" deep. Next cut notch for bone to fit in. This must be a snug fit. On other side I fit in two thin plastic strips mostly for looks but they do keep strings from wearing notches in wood. Three and one quarter inches of this block need be left this deep. The ends may now be cut very thin and each end taperd off. Center of piece is hollowed out so strings may be wrapped around. Holes must be drilled for strings. Use bit just large enough to let strings pass through. Lay bridge on face board where it will go and mark for strings. Now

BRIDGE SIZE AND DESIGN

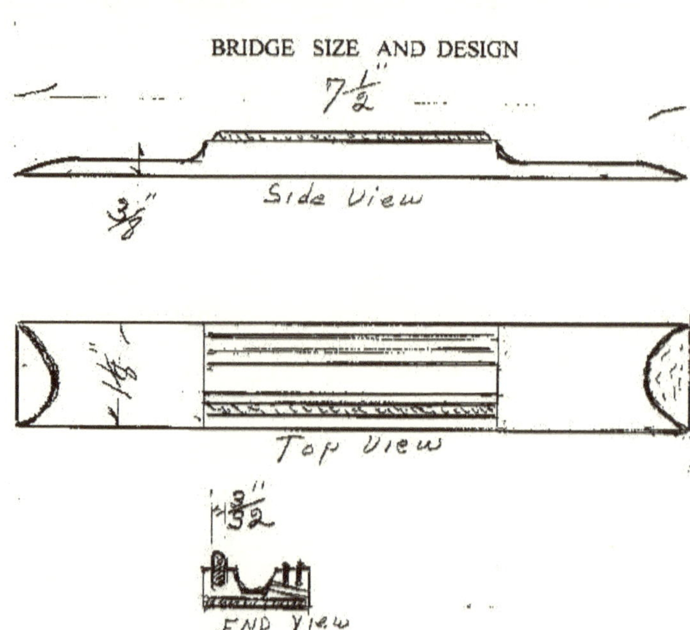

you must drill for strings and have this job done before bridge is glued on face. Also, if bridge is to be stained it must be done before it is glued on. In fact I completely finish the bridge before I install it on guitar. Bridge must be made to fit guitar face. Use scraper to remove wood and at the last lay sand paper—sand side up on sound board and rub bridge back and forth to get perfect fit. Mark where bridge will go and finish guitar before bridge is glued on.

EASY WAY TO FINISH A GUITAR

We started out to do things the easy way and so with the finish. I have made many fine guitars with no stain and no wood filler. The finish I use is just clear shellac. I put aside all the fine instructions about French polish and apply a thin coat of shellac with a small brush. Let it dry, at last twenty four hours. Shellac is slow to set so if you are too quick with the next coat you will just take off first coat. Sand very lightly between coats. Apply only enough to have wood covered. Do not put shellac on thick, the thinner will just dissolve what is already there. Use three coats or more. You can tell by looking at job. With this method you can check for bad

Glad Schwesinger

POLISHING WITH STEEL WOOL

spots. Small hole or grain that needs filling. These spots can be fixed, in fact with this method the finish can be reworked any time. When shellac has set it is time to polish. I use 000 steel wool. Watch the high gloss come off and a very soft beautiful finish appear. Turn the instrument in the light and you can see any bright glossy places that need more polishing. Shellac will bring out the beauty of the wood. It is like magic. That is why I use no stain and no filler. Anyone can do this, it takes only a little work and time. Factory guitars are sprayed with a heavy coat of lacquer. The finish is put on so thick they can polish with a power wheel with no worry of going through the finish. That thick coat does kill tone, many factory guitars can have tone improved simply by scraping finish off of sound board. Remember, shellac is slow to set so do not set guitar down, it will smudge the finish. Hang this instrument up for a week and let it hang. Now you can handle the guitar so now install the tuning heads. If finish is filling holes where rollers go then you must clear them. Screws are put in to hold them and you are ready for next step. Bridge and nut must be correct height. Notches must be cut in nut for strings. Make outside notches one eighth from edge of fret board and space the others evenly. Bridge must be glued on. Careful to get it on center and twenty five inches from nut to bridge. I hold it in place with very light pressure from clamps. When glue is dry, you should check frets again for even. File high ones down and use fret file to round off top again. I knew I would forget something. Fret file, Your guitar supply shop will sell you one and you do want the frets to look nice and more important, the instrument to play well. It takes time and work to get strings properly adjusted. Stay with it for no matter how good the sound no one will wish to play the guitar if it is hard to play. Get those strings down as low as possible without a buzzing on next fret. As the guitar ages it will sound better. A guitar has such a nice sound. I like the sound of a guitar.

A FEW GOOOD TIPS

1 - Have a small rug to place on work bench. This will prevent scratches on wood. Very important.

2 - Use table saw as work bench when fitting face and back to sides. With sides in outside mold fit both face and back. Then fasten sound board first, back after neck is fastened.

3 - When making fret board consider making it thinner on end next to box. Almost 1/4" at head end and 1/16" thinner at box end.

4 - Make place to hang guitar while finish is drying. It needs 24 hours

between coats and three days after last coat of shellac before it is polished with 000 steel wool.

5 - All wood which is to be bent on heat iron must be wet. Soak in water all night and ad water as you are bending. Water steaming through the wood is the secret to not cracking wood. Wood bent this way will hold that shape. Thus no strain on finished instrument.

6 - When setting strings I use a thin guitar pick as gage. I slide pick on first fret and under string. When pick touches string then string is low enough.

SOME HANDY INFORMATION

In the city of Tacoma Washington are the Guild of American Luthiers. Address as follows

Guild of American Luthiers

8222 South Park—Tacoma W A 98498
(206) 472—7853 Web page www. Luth.org

These folks sell plans—have ads for instrument wood and instrument parts and articles of builders which are of interest. To join is a very nominal fee and members receive a quarterly magazine. Many years ago I did receive their magazine and did even show one of my guitars at their convention in San Francisco. Year of 1980. They have adds for guitar supply outlets for the purchase of fret wire, plans, finishes and such. They are nice folks with just a lot of information.

The object of this book is to enable a first time builder to make a good sounding, good looking and easy playing guitar. Luck be with you.

OTHER INSTRUMENTS

There are many musical instruments made of wood. As I am a wood worker and not a musician I have gotten much pleasure building musical instruments. Of course I made many Steel string guitars. I did use an Old Martin for a model. Finished instruments were Dreadnought size. Some builders are purists and do not like steel strings but I like them and so I build both steel string and nylon string guitars.

Also the builder should know, guitars are made of many different woods. A logger friend brought me some quilted Maple and asked, will you make me a guitar of this wood? It had problems because of a tendency to chip but the finished instrument was outstanding. I made a few guitars of Alaska Cedar. One of the best sounding steel string guitars I ever made was Alaska Cedar back and sides with a Sitka Spruce face board. I have seen a few good guitars with Red Cedar face board but it is a bit to soft for my liking. A builder can look about and see what is available.

I made one flat iron Mandolin. I heard one being played and did like it. My Father played the mandolin and as a child I was thrilled when he played and it did seem like he could make that mandolin talk. I went to a local music store with paper, pencil and ruler. I measured the mandolin there and went home and built it. I was lucky—it sounds good, plays good and looks good. One of the old time fiddlers heard it and asked if he could borrow it for a night. He took the instrument to one of the shows they put on and did play it. I was so proud.

When I was in San Francisco the good wife bought me a plan for building an Irish Harp. That was one of the larger projects. The folks who sold the plans also sold the tuners and strings and such. Parts cost me another $60.00. Had to make a mold to bend box wood on.

Made the box of three ply glued together. Center ply was cross grain of other two. Used Alaska cedar for two layers and very thin Mahogany for center ply. Sound board was three ply with Sitka Spruce for two ply and Mahogany for cross grain center ply. All wood very thin. Tone was fine.

One senior dance that wife and I went to there was a musician who played a Marimba. One dance I took a ruler and pencil and paper. Got measurements and went home and built a Marimba. That took a long time. The musicians would not believe it could be built of any wood other than Rosewood. I used Sitka Spruce. One evening they showed up at my house to check this instrument I had built. They were truly surprised for the Spruce wood Marimba sounded all O K.

About the most simple instrument to build is the Appalachian Dulcimer. I have a book with plans for this instrument. It was easy to build and easy to play. I do not understand why we do not see and hear more of them. Building instruments has been a fine hobby. I have given away so many and it is so good when I hear some young person playing the guitar I gave them. Then I feel I have done a good thing. I do hope some one will read this book and enjoy to build their own instrument.

Glad Schwesinger

A LOGGER FRIEND BROUGHT QUILTED MAPLE
ASKED—GLAD WILL YOU BUILD GUITAR

CURING OF WOOD

Some folks think that the violin makers of old had the wood curing for many years. In all truth wood may be air dried and cured in twelve months. However, that is rushing things so if you buy a Spruce block I would advise splitting off a few boards and setting them aside to cure. After these boards are made only three thirty seconds thick they will dry faster. If they are where the air is damp they will also take up water faster. Caution, do not glue braces on until boards are completely dry. Same is true of back boards. Also, thin boards will tend to warp out of straight. It is best to place weight on boards to hold them flat while they cure.

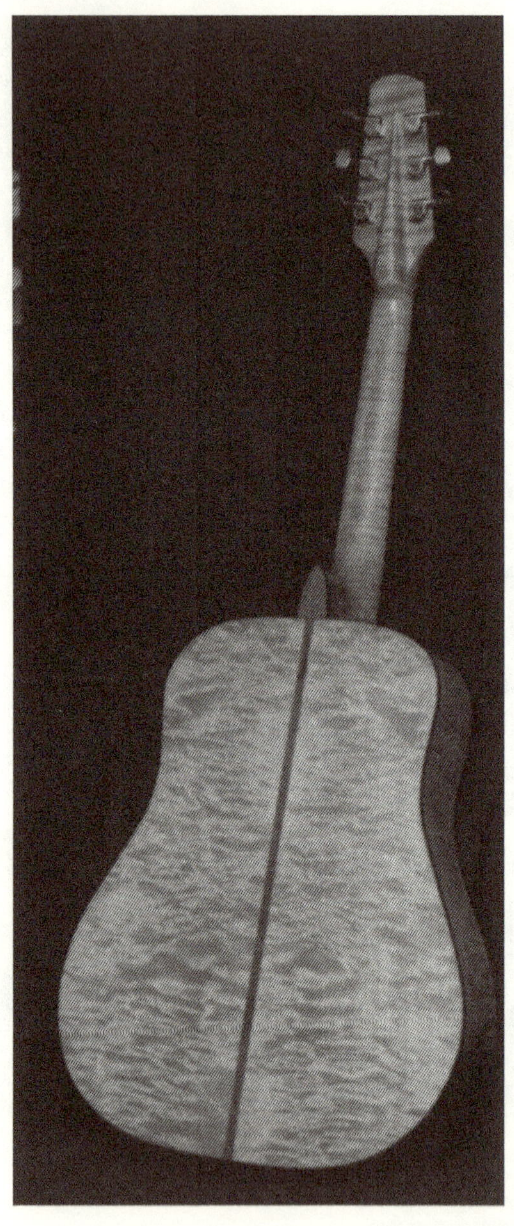

ABOUT THE AUTHOR

Glad is a retired shipwright. He has worked with wood all his life. Glad is now 83 years old and still very active, playing golf and ballroom dancing twice a week. He has just finished building a guitar.

Guitar building is just one of his hobbies. He has built Appalachian Dulcimers, Marimba, and a flat iron mandolin. He gives these instruments away. If he accepted money, he feels that would make it like a job. His instruments are located as far away as the East coast even Hawaii.